Friendship Fun
for
All Seasons

Friendship Fun for All Seasons

Great Ideas for Outdoor Adventures

by Lori Stacy

SCHOLASTIC INC.
New York Toronto London Auckland Sydney
Mexico City New Delhi Hong Kong

Special thanks to:
Leslie Finical, curator of the
Dallas Arboretum, for sharing her awesome
knowledge of plants and trees.

ISBN 0-439-16108-8

12 11 10 9 8 7 6 5 4 3 2 1   0 1 2 3 4 5/0

Cover designed by Louise Bova

Printed in the U.S.A.
First Scholastic printing, May 2000

TABLE OF CONTENTS

FALL

WINTER

INTRODUCTION

There's nothing better than being outside with your friends for excitement and adventure. Just think — you can explore nature, do outdoor arts and crafts, play sports, or go on long bike rides with your buds. This book has ideas for every season, beginning with spring and continuing through winter, to keep you and your friends having fun all year long. For each month, you'll get lots of great suggestions, including:

Do It! Awesome outdoor activities and nature walks

Make It! Recipes to celebrate the season

Create It! Crafts inspired by nature

and **Play It!** Great games for outdoors

So if you're ready for adventure, read on!

SPRING

Chapter One

March

March is a great month to . . .

※ make a rain gauge by drawing measurement marks on the outside of a clean glass jar, and placing it outside to see just how much rain the spring brings.

※ take a trip to your local zoo.

※ paint a terra-cotta pot green and plant clover inside, in honor of St. Patrick's Day.

👟 DO IT! Animal Discovery Nature Walks

With spring in the air, animals everywhere will be out to greet the warmer weather. Now's the perfect time to take long walks to observe the animal life around you.

It's likely to still be cold in most parts of the country, so be sure to dress warmly. Spring showers mean muddy paths, so you may want to wear waterproof shoes or boots.

Keep an eye out for little creatures beginning to emerge from their winter slumbers, like spiders and insects. Creepy as some of them may seem, many insects and spiders have a good purpose in nature. Some spiders feed on destructive insects, and some insects pollinate plants. See how many different types of insects and spiders you can find while on your nature walk.

Discover where these little creatures live (like underneath rocks or leaves) and whether they are loners or prefer to be in packs. You can bring along a book on bugs to help identify what it is you've found, or you can start a nature journal and draw pictures inside and look up your discoveries when you get home. (See the information about nature journals on page six.)

But don't just look down at the ground on your walk — look around! Since the trees are only just starting to get their leaves, it should be easy to spot birds' nests in them. Look up in the trees to see if you spy any birds' nests.

You can record your finds in your nature journal.

MAKE IT! Take-it-with-you Trail Mix

Trail mix got its name because it is a high-energy food that's easy to pack and take along on walks, hikes, or camping trips. There is no one particular recipe — you can throw together all sorts of ingredients to make the trail mix that's right for you. Before you go out in nature, get your friends together to make the trail mix. Then pack your snacks in plastic bags and keep them inside your pockets or your backpacks for a quick, easy pick-me-up.

Here are some ingredients you can choose from for your trail mix:

- Nuts
- Sunflower seeds
- Pretzel sticks or Goldfish crackers
- Cereal, such as Kix or Cheerios
- Dried fruit, like apples, bananas, or apricots
- Raisins
- Coconut flakes
- Candy, such as M&Ms
- Chocolate chips

Mix the ingredients together in a large bowl then place inside individual baggies.

CREATE IT! Outdoor Clubhouse

The first sign of spring will have you and your friends wanting to spend more time outdoors. Creating a clubhouse will get you back outside with shelter to keep you warm. And if it's still too cold outside, you can build your clubhouse indoors or in a garage.

Create a Yearlong Nature Journal

Make your nature experiences memorable by creating a nature journal. A nature journal can be as simple as a store-bought notebook or notepad, or as fancy as a notebook that you and your friends make or decorate.

As you explore nature throughout the year, keep track of where you go and what you see. Be sure to date each entry so you can compare your discoveries throughout the year. You can draw pictures of birds and other animals that you notice, or describe the trees you see at different times of year to note how they change each season.

Write down other things you observe, such as insects and spiders, ponds, streams, or interesting rocks. Collect leaves or flowers and paste them on pages inside your journal.

At the end of the year, you'll have a terrific nature scrapbook!

A clubhouse is a place that you and your friends can create and call your own. You can decorate it any way you'd like, play games inside, and come up with secret passwords or handshakes needed to enter.

You can build a simple or a fancy clubhouse depending on the materials you have available and your own personal taste. If you have big plans, you might need a grown-up helper. Be on the lookout for items to use in building your clubhouse, such as:

- Large cardboard boxes
- Tents or sheets
- Long sticks or wooden posts
- A blanket or sheets
- Tree branches

In selecting an outdoor area for your clubhouse, you might want to find a place that's close to a fence or wall. Create the clubhouse by using sticks or wooden posts and then draping tents or sheets over the posts. Or you can cut the top off a large box and turn it upside down. (Keep an eye out for neighbors who get a new refrigerator — there's no better box for a clubhouse than a huge refrigerator box!) You can then cut windows and a door out of the cardboard. You can make your clubhouse even larger by getting more than one box and placing them alongside each other. Have a grown-up help you cut out doors to go from one box to the other.

After you have your structure together, you can decorate it by painting pictures on the outside and inside walls, placing potted flowers outside the front door, and taping or tacking pieces of fabric or old sheets above the windows as curtains. You can make a door to the clubhouse with a piece of fabric. Inside, make furniture out of old crates or small logs.

With your clubhouse up and decorated, you and your friends will never want to leave!

🏀 PLAY IT! Around the World

It's basketball season, and there's no better time to be out on the courts. So grab a ball and your pals, and play a game of Around the World. You only need two or more players for this game, plus access to a basketball hoop and a court. Before you begin, you'll need to decide on seven spots around the basketball hoop to serve as shooting places. Mark the spots with chalk or tape, and then number them from one through seven.

Come up with an order of players. The first player begins the game by standing on spot number one and trying to throw the basketball into the hoop. If she makes it, she moves on to spot number two and tries it from there. When she misses, she ends her turn and goes to the end of the line.

The second player then starts at spot number one and tries to see how far she can get before missing a shot. After all the players have had their first turn, the first player gets to go again. She should start at the spot where she missed from the last turn, and she doesn't get to move to the next spot until she has made a basket from that spot. The player who makes her shots from all seven spots first has been "around the world" and wins the game.

Chapter Two

April

April is a great month to . . .

- ☀ *fly a kite.*
- ☀ *practice your softball swings at a local batting cage.*
- ☀ *plant a tree for Arbor Day.*
- ☀ *make a trip to a recycling center in honor of Earth Day — and bring along a bag full of newspapers, cans, and bottles to donate.*

👟 DO IT! Discover Spring Flowers on a Nature Walk

With spring flowers in bloom, you and your buds are in for one of the best nature walks of the year. Grab your nature journal

Searching for Four-Leaf Clovers

Four-leaf clovers are symbols of good luck. Even centuries ago, people considered them a charm against evil spirits. Four-leaf clovers are rare, because the plant that produces them mainly produces clover with three leaves. But with a little effort, you might just be able to find one!

and go on a hunt for wildflowers!

Before you begin, find out what wildflowers grow in your part of the country. You can browse through a nature guidebook, ask a local librarian, or search Web sites like *www.garden.com*. Depending on where you live, you may be able to spot wildflowers such as bluebonnets, which are common in Texas, dandelions, poppies, coneflowers, and daisies. Also, you can find out your state flower by checking an encyclopedia.

In the spring, bulbs that have been "resting" underground through the cold winter finally begin to bloom. Look for flowers such as tulips, daffodils, and crocuses that are just coming out of their winter slumbers.

After you are armed with info about your area's flora, take a nature walk and try to identify as many wildflowers as you can. If your state flower is a wildflower that blooms in the spring, you can try to find and identify it, too! Also, look for trees that are beginning to blossom. Try to identify the different trees you see in bloom.

Record your finds in your nature journal. You can even place a few flower petals right in the pages to press and preserve.

MAKE IT! Daisy Cookies

What you need:

- 20 large marshmallows
- 1 dozen sugar cookies (you can buy refrigerated cookie dough, packaged cookies, or make them from scratch)

- ◆ Tube of yellow icing
- ◆ Container of green frosting
- ◆ A grown-up to help you

Utensils:

- ◆ Kitchen scissors or knife
- ◆ Spreading knife
- ◆ Cookie sheet

What you do:

1. Bake the cookies according to the recipe on the package, and let them cool completely.

2. Use kitchen scissors or a knife to snip each marshmallow into 5 slices (or petals). (You may need a few extra for practice.) Put the snipped marshmallows to the side.

3. Lay all your cooled cookies on a clean, smooth surface. Spread each one with a thin layer of green frosting.

4. For each cookie, arrange 5 marshmallow petals in the shape of a flower and press them carefully onto the frosted cookie.

5. To finish, carefully fill the center of the "flower" with yellow icing.

Makes one dozen daisy cookies.

CREATE IT! Dried Flowers

Preserve flowers that you find by drying and pressing them. If done correctly, dried flowers can last for years.

What you need:

- Flowers (smaller flowers are easier to dry and preserve)
- Waxed paper or a plastic-covered photo album page
- A thick phone book
- A heavy object to keep flowers pressed, such as a cast-iron skillet or a brick

What you do:

1. Place the flowers between two sheets of waxed paper or underneath the plastic lining of the photo album page.

2. Place the waxed paper or photo album page inside the bottom pages of the phone book. Close the phone book and place a heavy object, such as a cast-iron skillet or a brick, on top to keep the flowers pressed.

3. Your flowers will dry best if kept in a warm, dry place. Check on their progress after a week. After they've dried, keep them in your memory album, or place them between the pages of your journal. You can also insert them behind the glass of a pretty picture frame.

🏀 PLAY IT! "Speed" Wiffle Ball

Celebrate the start of baseball season with a game of Wiffle ball with your buds. Wiffle ball is a lot like baseball and softball, but instead of using a hard baseball or soft-ball and gloves, you play Wiffle ball without gloves, using a plastic bat and ball. You can find Wiffle ball sets at most sporting goods or discount stores.

Teams switch places after three players have had their turns at bat (whether they are called "out" or not). By playing the game this way, the innings will be much shorter and the game will be more exciting.

You'll need a large grassy area or a baseball diamond. If there aren't bases already, mark bases with old towels, rags, or shirts. You'll also need to mark a pitching mound.

Select teams with equal numbers of players. Each team should have at least three players. After you have selected the teams, toss a coin to see which team will be at bat first. The team who wins the toss should choose to be in the outfield first so they'll have the last chance to score at bat.

The outfield team will need a pitcher and fielders to stand in different positions around the field, such as at first base and a shortstop who's positioned between second and third bases. If you have enough players, you can have players at second and third base as well.

If there are enough players, the outfield

team should also choose a player as the catcher. If there are not enough players, then the team that's at bat can have one of their players be the catcher. An umpire is needed to call the plays. If you can, have a grown-up or a friend who isn't playing be the umpire. If not, the catcher can double as the umpire.

The team that's at bat should come up with a lineup of batters. The first person in the lineup bats first. The game begins when the pitcher throws the ball (the pitch should be underhanded). The player on the team who is at bat stands at one side of home plate holding the bat.

When it reaches her, she then swings at the ball, trying to hit it. If she hits the ball, she should drop the bat and begin to run toward first base. If she swings and misses the ball, it's called a strike and she can try again. Unless the pitches are not good (the umpire calls the pitch good or bad), and the batter does not swing, she is out after making three strikes.

If the player hits the ball and starts to run toward first base, the outfielders go after the ball and try to throw it to the girl at first base before the runner gets there, or they can tag (touching the runner while holding the ball) the runner out as she is running to second or third base. If the ball is hit into the air, the outfielders can also make an out by catching the ball before it hits the ground. If the batter makes it to first base, she can choose to try to make it to second or third base. Or, if the hit is good enough, the batter can try for a home run by running around all the bases without being tagged out. If she chooses to stay on a base, she can advance toward home base after another player hits the ball. The winning team is the one that has the most points after nine innings.

Chapter Three

May

May is a great month to . . .

❀ *visit a local farmers' market and sample the season's best fruits and vegetables.*

❀ *plant your own outdoor vegetable and flower garden.*

❀ *make your mom happy by creating a lovely Mother's Day bouquet of fresh flowers.*

❀ *visit a botanical garden to see the spring flowers.*

👟 DO IT! Carnival Fun

Make believe the carnival has rolled in to town by creating your own set of carnival games. Come up with "prizes" for the games, such as candies or small plastic toys and games. Here are some examples.

Ring Toss

You'll need old empty bottles with long necks, as well as "rings" to toss at the bottles. If you don't have plastic rings (like from a swimming pool game or a child's toy), then you can make them by cutting rings out of cardboard. Just be sure that the cardboard is heavy and sturdy and that the opening of the ring fits easily over the bottles.

To set up your ring toss, arrange the bottles in a pattern on the grass. Mark a line a few feet back from the bottles for your friends to stand behind. Give each player three rings to try to toss over the bottles. Prizes go to players who get all three rings over the necks of the bottles.

Ping-Pong Ball Toss

Fill small bowls or fishbowls with water and arrange them on the ground. Mark a line a few feet from where the bowls are.

Give each player three plastic Ping-Pong balls and let her try to toss a ball into one of the bowls of water. If all three balls land in the water without falling out, your friend gets a prize!

Penny Toss

As with the Ping-Pong ball toss, your friends will need to land their pennies in a dish in order to win at this game. Arrange small glass plates or saucers on the ground. If you can't get glass plates, you can use small paper plates (it just won't sound as good when the pennies land!).

Mark a line a few feet back from where the plates are; the farther back you are, the harder it will be. You may want to try it out close at first; you can move the line back if it is too easy. Give each player five pennies and see how many she can get to land and stay in the dishes. Award prizes to the players who get three or more pennies in the dishes.

✋ MAKE IT! Chocolate-dipped Animal Crackers

Your carnival celebration just wouldn't be complete without a treat for the attendees. Jazz up animal crackers a bit by dipping them in melted chocolate or candy coating and then topping them with candy sprinkles.

What you need:

- 1 or 2 small boxes of animal crackers
- 4 ounces semisweet chocolate (⅔ cup chocolate chips or 4 one-ounce blocks)
- Colored candy sprinkles
- A grown-up to help you

Utensils:

- Saucepan
- Tongs
- Waxed paper

What you do:

1. Melt the chocolate in the saucepan over low heat and then remove from heat (with a grown-up's help).

2. Using the tongs, dip each cracker into the melted chocolate, keeping the head of the animal out of the chocolate.

3. Lay the chocolate-dipped crackers on a sheet of waxed paper. Before the chocolate hardens, sprinkle candy sprinkles over the chocolate. Turn the crackers over and sprinkle the other side.

4. Allow the crackers to cool completely, then serve!

Makes enough for 2–4 friends.

CREATE IT! Sidewalk Art

Now that the weather's warmed up, it's time to hit the pavement — literally! Sidewalk chalk, which is thicker than normal chalk, is easier to use outside, but any chalk can be used to create drawings on the ground. Find a paved or concrete area that has no traffic and is free of oil or grease. Create pictures using the chalk, or work together with your friends to come up with a street mural.

For your mural, come up with an idea or a theme, like underwater life, a "summer fun" scene, or a portrait of all your friends. Before you start drawing, talk about the size of your mural and what it is going to look like. Make sure each artist is responsible for her area of the mural, then get to work creating your masterpiece!

Easy-to-Make Eggshell Chalk

You can create your own sidewalk chalk using eggshells and food coloring.

What you need:
- 6 eggshells, washed and dried
- 1 teaspoon hot water

- 1 teaspoon flour
- A drop of food coloring (1 color per recipe)

Utensils:

- Mortar and pestle to grind eggshells into powder (or a blender or food processor)
- Strainer or sifter
- Small bowl
- Medium-sized bowl
- Measuring spoons
- Paper towels

What you do:

1. Grind the eggshells into a powder using a mortar and pestle (or, with a grown-up's help, grind the eggshells in a blender or food processor). Place the ground eggshells into a fine strainer or sifter and then sift them into a small bowl, keeping out any large pieces of eggshell.
2. Mix together the water and flour to

make a paste (you can add more flour or water to create more paste, if needed). Add 1 tablespoon eggshell powder (and food coloring, if desired). Stir the mixture together; it should be in the form of a thick paste.

3. Shape the mixture into a large stick of chalk, and roll it up tightly in a paper towel. Let it dry in a warm, dry place for about two to three days. The chalk should be completely dry before you use it.

Use this homemade sidewalk chalk outside on pavement or sidewalks only.

🏀 PLAY IT! Four-Square and Two-Square

You and your friends will have a ball playing four-square and two-square.

Four-Square

Like the name says, you'll need four squares — and four or more players — for this game. You'll also need chalk and a playground ball that will bounce (like a kickball or a tennis ball). Play this game on pavement so that the ball will bounce.

Before you begin, draw a large square on the pavement. It should be about 20 feet long on each side, or about four body lengths long. After you have drawn the large square, divide it into four boxes by drawing a line across the middle from each side. (At some parks and playgrounds, there are four-square areas already painted on the pavement.)

Begin with four players, one standing in each of the squares. Select a player to go first. She starts the game by serving the ball from the back of her square. To serve, she bounces the ball once in her square, then hits it underhand with one or two open hands so that it lands in one of the other squares. The player whose square the ball bounces in must then hit it the same way to another of the squares. The players continue to bounce the ball back and forth to one another until one player is "out."

A player is out when she misses the ball, lets it bounce more than once in her square, hits it on the line, or hits it outside of another player's square. As soon as a player is out, she exits the game and another player comes into her square. The new player then gets to serve the ball and start the game over.

If there are only four players, you can select one square to be the "serving square." Players rotate clockwise into the serving square after each out, with the player who has been called out going to the end of the serving line.

Two-Square

If you have only two or three players, you can play two-square instead of four-square. Just draw two connected squares on the ground using chalk. Select the first two players to start, and of those, choose someone to serve.

Play the game the same way you play four-square — by bouncing the ball back and forth to each other. After one player is called out, she has to give up her square to the next player. When a player wins a round, she becomes the server.

SUMMER

Chapter Four

June

June is a great month to . . .

☀ *throw a pool party with your pals to celebrate the end of the school year.*

☀ *go catch dinner by fishing at a local fish farm.*

☀ *wash your dad's car for Father's Day.*

👟 DO IT! Camp Out

Warm summer months are the perfect time to spend a night outdoors with your pals. After the sun goes down, there's a whole new world of nature to see — even in the dark. Animals that stay undercover during the day come out to play, and instead of the sun, it's the stars and the moon that light up the land. Enjoy an evening outdoors by planning a camp-out with your pals.

While you may be lucky enough to have an overnight camping area near your home — an adventure you'd need a grown-up for — you can always experience the adventure of a camp-out in your own back-yard.

For your camp-out, you'll need a tent (especially if it's cool outside), plus sleeping bags, pillows, flashlights, bottles of water, and snacks for the "midnight munchies."

Before you hit the sack, sit outside and take in your surroundings. If it's a clear night, see who can be the first to find the Big Dipper or the Little Dipper among all the stars. Be on the lookout for falling stars — don't forget to make a wish if you spot one!

Listen closely and you might be able to hear crickets, who love to break up the night's silence with their chirping. Shine your flashlight their way and they'll go silent to keep you from finding their hiding place.

No camp-out would be complete without campfire tales. You and your friends can take turns telling stories — the scarier, the better!

After everyone is sleepy, turn the flashlights off and get some shut-eye.

MAKE IT! Rainbow Fruit Kabobs

Bring these back to your tent for a late-night snack.

What you need:
- An apple
- A banana
- A pear
- A cantaloupe
- Strawberries
- A can of pineapple chunks

Utensils:
- Knife
- Kabob Sticks

- ◆ A can opener
- ◆ A melon baller
- ◆ A large bowl
- ◆ A grown-up to help you

What you do:

1. Wash the fresh fruit.
2. Cut the apple, pear, and banana into one-inch chunks. Have a grown-up help you. Put the fruit pieces into the bowl.
3. Have your grown-up helper slice open the cantaloupe and remove the seeds. Use the melon baller to make balls of cantaloupe. Place the cantaloupe balls in the bowl.
4. Open the can of pineapple and put it in the bowl.
5. Have everyone take turns making kabobs. Slide the pieces of fruit onto the kabob sticks. Make your kabobs colorful by alternating fruits on each stick.

CREATE IT! Homemade Boats

You and your friends can create sailboats that really float using empty milk cartons and a few other easy-to-find household items.

What you need to make one boat:
- A clean, empty, pint-sized paper milk carton that's been cut down the middle lengthwise (you may want to have a grown-up cut the carton for you)
- Tape
- Four Popsicle sticks
- Cardboard
- Glue
- Cellophane wrap
- Scissors

What you do:

1. If you have the side of the carton with the open top, use tape to close the opening. Turn the carton over so that the outside is resting on the ground.

2. Cut a piece of cardboard into a strip that is one inch high and one inch longer than the width of the boat (about four inches).

3. Tape the strip of cardboard inside, across the middle of the boat so that it can be used as a base for the sail.

4. To assemble the sail, glue together three Popsicle sticks to form a triangle.

5. Attach the fourth Popsicle stick in the center of one side of the triangle, using glue.

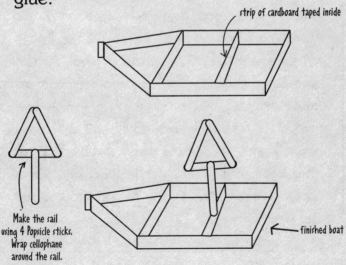

strip of cardboard taped inside

Make the sail using 4 Popsicle sticks. Wrap cellophane around the sail.

finished boat

6. After the glue has dried, cut a piece of cellophane wrap to the size of the triangle and attach it to the Popsicle sticks with tape. Fasten the sail to the boat by taping the base of the fourth popsicle stick to the cardboard strip inside the boat.

Your sailboat is ready to float!

Sailboat Races

After you and your friends have created boats, you can hold a boat race across a pond or pool. Place all the boats at one end of the pond or pool. After someone shouts "Go!" let your boats go and see who makes it to the finish line first. Try blowing on your sail or using your hands to create soft waves to push the boat. It'll take a little luck and some coaxing from the shore to get your boat to win.

🏀 PLAY IT! Summer Olympic Games

If you and your friends have all day to play, instead of settling on just a few games, take part in a bunch of races and games by creating your own outdoor Olympic Games competition!

First, decide on teams, or "countries." Each team should have at least three players. The teams can come up with clever names and figure out a way to show the others they're a team, like having each player tie the same-colored bandanna around her arm, or wearing matching baseball caps or T-shirts. Each team should also select a captain to lead the team and serve on the "Olympic Committee."

After each team has selected a captain, the Olympic Committee should meet to come up with all the games and races that will be part of the competition. You can hold races, relays, long-jump contests, bike races, and even swimming challenges.

Once you've come up with your list, it's time for the games to begin!

Teams compete against one another in all of the events. After an event, determine the first-, second-, and third-place winners. You can ask a grown-up to be the judge.

Award the first-place winner of each game with a "gold medal," and then award the silver and bronze medals to the second- and third-place winners. (You can create medals by cutting circles out of construction paper and coloring them gold, silver, and bronze, and attaching them to a string necklace. Or you can use coins as medals: quarters for gold, nickels for silver, and pennies for bronze.) Make the awarding of medals a celebration by having a member of the Olympic Committee call the winners up to the front of the group to present them with their honors.

Teams try to win the most medals — especially gold medals — during the games. After the games are complete, each team tallies up their totals by counting one point for each bronze medal, two points for each silver medal, and three points for each gold medal.

Wrap up the events with a "Closing Ceremony" — complete with snack prizes for all the athletes.

Chapter Five

July

July is a great month to...

❋ pick ripe, fresh cherries at a local cherry orchard.

❋ watch the fireworks at a local Fourth of July celebration.

❋ dip your feet into a pond or stream to cool off.

👟 DO IT! The Ultimate Bike Ride

What's the best way to get around town during the summer months? By bike, of course! Make it a day on wheels by planning a marathon bike ride and picnic.

Before you head off, plan your route. Get or make a map of the area you'll be covering. Be on the lookout for spots you'd like to stop and visit, like a pretty garden or even another pal's house. If you are required to stay near your home, you can still make the bike ride a long one by going up and down each street in the neighborhood.

Pack a healthy, high-energy lunch in a backpack or in a sack that will fit in your bike's basket. Fill your water bottles, and bring along extra if the weather is especially warm. Also take snacks like granola bars, carrot sticks, or fruit for breaks during the ride.

Be sure to dress appropriately for the weather, wearing layers of clothing if you think it might get warmer or cooler during your ride. (Remember, the more you ride, the warmer you will get.)

After you have done all the planning, it's time to take off. Play "follow the leader" as you ride, having each person in a single file line do just what the leader does (so long as it is safe). For instance, if the leader rides her bike up one driveway and down the next, all the girls following do the same thing. Take turns being the leader of the bike ride so that everyone gets a chance to be the leader.

Stop for water and snack breaks when you or your friends get tired, then take a lunch break at a park, field, or picnic area.

MAKE IT! Picnic Lunches

Picnic lunches are perfect for a daylong bike ride, or any time you and your friends want to enjoy life outdoors! When packing a picnic lunch, be sure to choose food that will stay fresh out of the refrigerator and that won't get soggy after too long. If you can, pack your picnic in a "cool pack."

Traditional Picnic Lunch

Make sandwiches out of hard rolls (like hoagie rolls), with cold cuts such as ham, turkey, roast beef, or salami. Add lettuce, tomatoes, and mustard. (Avoid mayonnaise because it can spoil.) Or pack peanut-butter sandwiches. Wrap the sandwiches tightly in plastic wrap, then cover in foil to keep them cool and free from moisture. If you have a cool pack, you can take along any kind of sandwich you like, such as tuna fish or cheese, because it won't spoil.

Bring along some fruit, like apples, oranges, or bananas, and fill small plastic bags with fresh-cut vegetables, chips, or cookies.

Wrap a cold bottle of water or a can of soda in foil to keep it cool, and add to your picnic lunch.

French Picnic Lunch

Sandwiches aren't your only option for a picnic lunch, especially if you have a cooler. Do as the French do and pack a hunk of bread, as well as slices of cheese, and, if you like, slices of salami. When it's time to eat, break off pieces of bread and eat with the cheese and salami.

To take your lunches along with you, pack them in a backpack or in bags that will fit in your bike's basket.

CREATE IT! Independence Day Bike Parade

Show your patriotism on the Fourth of July by creating a patriotic bike parade. Decorate your bikes in red, white, and blue using streamers, ribbons, flags, balloons, and other materials you find.

If you have a bike basket, you may want to add "noisemaking" equipment, like a tape player to play such patriotic tunes as "The Star-Spangled Banner" or "America the Beautiful." You can also ring your bike bells as you ride along.

Decide on a time and place to get together with your friends and parade through your neighborhood. If your community is holding an Independence Day parade, ask the organizers if you can be part of it. Then ride through town in your festive parade of bikes.

🏀 PLAY IT! Bike Races

You and your friends can stage your own biking competitions. For the two cycling events described below, you'll need to be in a paved area that's free of traffic. You may also want to bring along chalk to mark starting lines, finish lines, and other parts of the courses.

Tricycle Race

Someone in the neighborhood is sure to have toddlers. See if you and your friends can borrow two tricycles to compete in these wacky relay races. Select two teams with an even amount of players. The first player on each team should get on the tricycle behind the starting line. After someone yells "Go!" the first player from each team starts the race by riding across the finish line and then back to the start. As soon as she gets back, she gets off the tricycle and the second player gets on and does the same thing. The first team to finish the race wins.

Tightrope Race

In this race, riders pretend to be on a tightrope. To get the course ready, draw chalk lines — one for each team or player — from the starting line to the finish line. Each participant has to ride her bike from the starting line to the finish line while staying on the line. The first rider, or each person competing, lines up behind her chalk line at the starting line. At the sound of "Go!" each player starts to ride to the finish line while trying to keep both wheels of the bike on the chalk line. You'll find that it's more important to be slow and careful than it is to speed through this race. If you veer off the "tightrope," you're automatically out. Whoever stays on the line and finishes in the shortest amount of time wins.

Chapter Six

August

August is a great month to . . .

- ☀ *build a sand castle.*
- ☀ *read a book in the sun.*
- ☀ *stay cool at a water park.*

👟 DO IT! Hide the Water Gun

Don't be afraid to get wet playing this game — it's bound to happen to at least a few players! To play, you'll need a small water gun that's filled with water. You'll also need to come up with your playing area and a "home base" that players must run back to in order to be safe. You can select a tree or a lamppost to serve as home base. You'll need three or more players to play this game.

To begin, select a player to be "It" first and give her the water gun. Then have the rest of the players hide their eyes while waiting at home base. The player who's It then goes and hides the water gun. After she has hidden it, she yells "Ready!" to the other players, and they begin the search for the water gun.

The player who finds the water gun should try to carefully conceal it. It's up to her to try and squirt other players before they make it back to home base, otherwise she will be It. As soon as the other players see that she has the gun, they should try and run back to touch home base before they get squirted with water. The last player to get squirted with water before she touches home base is It. If none of the players get squirted, then the person who found the water gun is It and must hide the gun for the next round.

✋ MAKE IT! Homemade Ice Cream

You don't even need an ice cream maker to create this refreshing summer-time treat!

What you need (amounts are shown for each ice cream eater, so for you and two buds, you will need three of each item listed below):

- 1 small plastic bag that seals
- 1 large plastic bag that seals
- ½ cup milk
- 1 tablespoon sugar
- ¼ teaspoon vanilla
- ¼ cup salt (rock salt or regular salt)
- Ice cubes
- Measuring cups
- Measuring spoons

What you do:

1. Fill the large bag halfway with ice cubes, then add ¼ cup salt.

2. Place the milk, sugar, and vanilla in the small bag. Seal the small bag tightly and place inside the large bag of ice.

3. Seal the large bag, then shake it or turn it for 5 to 10 minutes, until the contents in the small bag are solid. You may want to take turns shaking the bag so your hands don't get too cold! Also, you shouldn't do this in the hot sun, since the ice will melt before the ice cream freezes.

4. Remove the small bag from the large bag, wipe away any excess salt from the opening of the small bag, open, and enjoy!

CREATE IT! Make Your Own Sundial

Before clocks and watches existed, people kept track of the time of day by using a sundial. Take advantage of this sunny month by creating your own sundial.

What you need:
- ◆ Paper plate
- ◆ A straw
- ◆ A ruler
- ◆ Scissors
- ◆ Tape
- ◆ A marker or pen

What you do:

1. Turn the paper plate upside down. Using a ruler, draw a line on the paper plate from one end of the plate to the center.

2. Carefully poke a hole through the center of the plate using the scissors, then insert the straw through the middle.

3. Tilt the straw so that it is leaning over the line you drew, then secure it in place by taping the straw at the top of the hole and on the bottom of the plate.

4. At exactly noon, take the sundial outside and face it so that the shadow of the

straw falls directly on the line. Secure the sundial to a flat area on the ground (you can use tape or a few rocks to keep it in place) and mark the number 12 next to the line.

5. At each hour of the day, mark a line on the sundial where the shadow falls and write what time of day it is next to the line. Now you'll be able to tell what time it is by looking at where the shadow falls!

🏀 PLAY IT! In-line Skate-a-thon

With warm, sunny weather in nearly every part of the country, August is the perfect month to "shine" in dance routines performed on skates. Pretend that you and your friends are figure skaters competing for an Olympic gold medal as you come up with your artistic acts.

You can compete individually or as a pair with another skater. Find a paved area that's free of traffic to create and practice your routines. If you have a portable tape or CD player, you can choreograph a performance to music. Try to incorporate turns, fancy arm movements, and leg lifts as you develop your routine.

When each skater or pair has come up with a routine, it's time to stage the competition. Ask grown-ups or other friends to serve as judges in the event. Perform your routines in front of the judges and have them score each competitor by giving her or the pair a score of 1 to 10, with 10 being the best. Total each competitor's scores.

After all the competitors have done their routines, whoever has the highest score is declared the winner.

Be Safe on Skates

Follow these tips to stay safe while you skate:

1. Wear protective gear. Chances are, you're going to fall at some point. Wearing full-protective gear – a helmet, wrist pads, elbow pads, and knee pads – can spare you from getting hurt.

2. Be a careful student. Learn to skate in a paved area that's free of traffic, hills, and other obstacles.

3. Watch your speed. It's hard to stop quickly on in-line skates, so be careful not to go too fast in areas that may require you to come to an immediate stop.

4. Avoid hills. It's easy to go from slow to out of control while skating, so beware of hills – big or small.

FALL

Chapter Seven

September

September is a great month to . . .

🌞 *visit an apple orchard and pick a basketful of fall's best apples.*

🌞 *cheer on a local school's football team at a game.*

🌞 *go on a horseback ride.*

👟 DO IT! Photographic Nature Walk

Autumn is one of the most beautiful times of year. In cooler climates, leaves are turning magnificent colors and beginning to fall. Warmer climates get a second chance at spring color, as rain and cooler weather revive grass, plants, and flowers. No matter where you live, it's a great time of year to capture nature on film. It's easy and fun to take pictures outdoors, and with all the inexpensive one-use cameras out there, you don't even need to own fancy equipment.

Get a camera, grab your friends, and follow these tips to get your best shots:

1. Don't shoot directly into the sun. It's best for the sun to be behind you (but watch out not to get your own shadow in the shot!).

2. Get a little closer. Try to get close to things like flowers and plants. Instead of shooting a bunch of flowers, try taking a picture of just one.

3. Create a "frame" for your shot. If you are shooting from far back, try to get the limbs of a nearby tree or plant in the foreground of your picture to make it more special.

4. Try shooting at different times of day. Outdoor light is different throughout the

day because of the angle of the sun. Sneak an early morning shot or try to capture an image at sunset.

5. Don't disturb the animals. Photograph animals as they are, instead of trying to get their attention. Stay a safe distance from them and try not to disturb them — you'll get a better picture if they don't know you're taking one!

✋ MAKE IT! Maple Apple Crunch

Apples are at their best in the fall, and they taste great paired with maple syrup, as in this yummy dessert.

What you need:

- 8 to 10 graham crackers
- ½ cup melted, cooled butter
- 4 apples, peeled, cored, and sliced
- ⅓ cup pure maple syrup
- Vanilla ice cream (optional)
- A grown-up to help you

Utensils:
- ◆ Large plastic bag that seals
- ◆ Measuring spoons
- ◆ Measuring cups
- ◆ Wooden spoon
- ◆ 8"×8"×2" glass baking dish
- ◆ A rolling pin (optional)

What you do:

1. Preheat oven to 325° F.

2. Place the graham crackers in the bag, seal, and use your fists or a rolling pin to crush the graham crackers. Add the melted butter to the bag and mix together inside the bag.

3. Place the apples in the baking dish and pour the maple syrup over them. Stir in the graham cracker mix, then place inside the oven and bake for 25 minutes.

Serve with the vanilla ice cream, if you wish. Makes 6 servings.

CREATE IT! Tree Branch Frames

Use branches from trees to create a frame that will let you bring the outdoors inside. It's a great way to display your nature photos!

What you need:

- An inexpensive, wooden frame with narrow edges
- Assorted branches
- Wood glue

What you do:

1. You and your friends will need to collect tree branches before you begin this project. Try to find branches that are flat and straight, as they will be easier to fasten to the frame. You will need to break some of the branches so that they are the same length or width as the frame.

2. Lay your branches on top of the frame to figure out what looks best before you attach them.

3. Glue the branches onto the frame. Let the glue dry before adding a picture and putting your frame back together.

4. If you'd like, you can attach other items from nature onto the frame as well, such as acorns, pebbles, or leaves.

🏀 PLAY IT! Blindman's Bluff

Think you could spot your friends with your eyes closed? Blindman's Bluff will put you to the test. In this game, you need to rely on your sense of touch to identify other players. You'll need at least four players to play the game, and a bandanna or cloth to tie over a player's eyes.

Before you begin, select a player to be "It." Tie the bandanna around her eyes so that she cannot see. Then form a circle around her. Have her begin the game by spinning in a circle as she counts to three. After she counts to three, she should stop and then point directly in front of her. Whoever is standing closest to where she has pointed has to walk up to her. It's up to the player who is It to try to figure out, without looking, who is standing in front of her. The only sense she'll be able to rely on is her sense of touch. She can touch the other player's hair and face. She then must guess who it is. If she guesses correctly, the player in front of her becomes It. If she guesses incorrectly, the person must identify who she is, and the player who's It must repeat her turn until she is able to correctly identify a player standing before her.

Chapter Eight

October

October is a great month to...

❋ rake fallen leaves into huge piles, then jump in them.

❋ pick out perfect pumpkins at an outdoor pumpkin patch.

❋ hold a contest with your friends to see who can create the spookiest jack-o'-lantern.

👟 DO IT! Our Town

October is a month that's made for make-believe. After all, it's the month of Halloween. One way you can put your imagination to work is by playing "Our Town."

Pretend that you and your friends live in a world where bicycles are cars and then choose an area that will be your "home." That's all you need to do to get your imagination started and play Our Town. Then it's up to you and your friends to come up with the rest of the story!

To start, each of you should pick out your home: It can be your front porch, an area at the side of your house, or your backyard. Take out your bike to use as a car. Get together with your friends and have everyone describe what their imaginary house and car look like.

Then come up with a nearby location for your "workplace," and determine what line of work you are in. Pretend to go about your "normal" activities — drive your "car" to work, meet up with your friends at your "house" or theirs, and talk about what's going on at your job and at home.

You and your friends will find that it's easy to let your imagination run free as you "live" in your made-up world!

🖐 MAKE IT! Toasted Pumpkin Seeds

Don't throw away all the goop inside the pumpkins you carve! There are tasty treats waiting to be made with all those pumpkin seeds.

What you need:
- A medium-size pumpkin
- Cookie sheet
- Cooking oil spray
- Newspaper
- A knife
- A colander
- Paper towels
- Wooden spoon, large spoon, or ice-cream scoop
- A grown-up to cut open the pumpkin

What you do:

1. Preheat the oven to 225° F.

2. Place the pumpkin on top of sheets of newspaper. Have a grown-up cut an opening at the top of the pumpkin.

3. Remove the top. Using a wooden spoon, ice-cream scoop, or your hand, clean out the insides of the pumpkin, removing all the seeds and pulp. Remove as many of the seeds from the pulp as you can, and place the seeds inside the colander.

4. Rinse the seeds to remove any remaining pulp.

5. Place the cleaned seeds on paper towels and pat them dry with more paper towels.

6. Spread the pumpkin seeds over a cookie sheet that's been sprayed with cooking oil spray, and bake the seeds in the oven for 1 to 2 hours, carefully mixing the seeds up with a wooden spoon every 15 minutes during baking, until they are evenly toasted. (Use pot holders to hold the cookie sheet while you are mixing the seeds or ask a grown-up to help.)

7. Let the seeds cool on the cookie sheet for a half hour to an hour, then serve.

Makes enough for 6–8 friends (depending on the size of the pumpkin).

🖌 CREATE IT! Fall Foliage Place Mats

Collect all kinds of colored leaves to make these beautiful fall place mats.

What you need:
- Assortment of leaves
- Waxed paper
- Iron and ironing board
- Towel
- Poster board in assorted fall colors
- Scissors
- Glue
- A grown-up to iron

What you do:

1. Cut waxed paper into 14-inch sheets. Cut two sheets of waxed paper for each place mat. Cut poster board into 14"×16" sheets.

2. Place some of the leaves in a single layer on one sheet of waxed paper that's

been laid on top of the ironing board. Place another sheet of waxed paper over the top.

3. Cover the waxed paper with a towel and ask a grown-up to gently iron to seal the waxed paper sheets together.

4. Let cool for 5 minutes, then glue onto the sheets of poster board.

🏀 PLAY IT! Pumpkin Races

October's cooler days make it the perfect month for holding a pumpkin race with your pals. Odd-shaped pumpkins, which you must roll down the field, make this game both fun and funny!

You can hold this race with just two competitors, or form relay teams with equal numbers of players if you are with a large group. Each competitor, or each team, will need a medium-to-large-size pumpkin to compete in the race.

You'll need to have an open, grassy area. Mark off or designate the starting line and the finish line. If you are competing as a relay, each team should decide the order that their players will run in the race. Alternate players at the starting line and the finish line (for instance, the second player should wait at the finish line to start her turn). Place a pumpkin in front of each runner.

After someone yells "Go!" runners must advance to the finish line while using their hands to roll the pumpkin in front of them. You'll soon find out that the pumpkins will want to go every which way but straight!

If it's a simple race to the finish, then the first person to cross the finish line with her pumpkin wins. If it's a relay, players must pass off the pumpkin to the next person on the team, who is waiting behind the finish line. The team whose final runner crosses the finish line first with the pumpkin wins the game.

Chapter Nine

November

November is a great month to . . .

☀ *plant tulip and daffodil bulbs outside for beautiful flowers in the spring.*

☀ *organize a "Turkey Walk" with your friends and family for a little post-Thanksgiving dinner exercise.*

☀ *make strings of fresh cranberries using a large needle and heavy thread, then hang them outdoors as a treat for the birds.*

👟 DO IT! Searching for Rocks

Although you may not be able to see too many plants with green leaves at this time of year, you can still discover other natural wonders while on a nature walk. Make it your mission to find and collect all sorts of rocks as you and your friends go on your walk.

Observe the colors, shapes, and sizes of rocks. See who can find the biggest rock and the smallest rock during the walk. You can also look for unusual rock formations.

Go near streams, ponds, or lakes to find rocks resting at the edge of the water. Try to find a few that are flat, to skim across the water's surface.

See if you and your friends can find rocks shaped liked familiar objects, such as an animal or a letter of the alphabet. Collect a few to use for art projects. Write descriptions of what you find in your journal.

MAKE IT! Rock Candy

It's easy to guess how this candy got its name — it not only looks like rocks, but it's hard as rocks, too!

What you need:
- ◆ 3 cups water
- ◆ 2 cups sugar
- ◆ Cooking oil spray
- ◆ Food coloring (optional)
- ◆ A grown-up to help you

Utensils
- ◆ Cookie sheet
- ◆ Heavy saucepan
- ◆ Measuring cup
- ◆ Large wooden spoon

What you do:
1. Spray the cookie sheet with the cooking oil spray.
2. Boil the water in the saucepan over high heat. Let boil 2 to 3 minutes, then add the sugar and stir until it's dissolved. Return the mixture to a boil and stir constantly until it begins to harden and form crystals.

3. Remove from the heat. After the mixture stops boiling, you can stir in one to two drops of food coloring, if you like.

4. Carefully pour the mixture onto the cookie sheet and let it cool completely. Once it's cooled, break into pieces and eat.

Makes about 10 servings.

Skimming Rocks

You can make rocks bounce across the top of the water's surface. The best rocks for skimming are those that are circular and flat, almost like a large coin or disk.

To skim rocks, hold the sides of a rock with your thumb and pointer finger. Fold your other fingers into a fist. Hold the rock so that it is flat, with your hand in front of your body and your elbow bent, then turn your wrist in.

Stand in front of the pond or lake. (It works best when the water is still.) You can also squat a bit so that when you throw the rock it will have a better chance of staying on top of the water.

When you are ready, quickly open your wrist and your arm as you release the rock straight in front of you. See how many times the rock bounces on top of the water before it sinks. It may take some practice, so collect a stack of rocks and don't give up.

CREATE IT! Painted Rocks

Turn ordinary rocks into works of art with a little paint and a lot of creativity!

What you need:

- An assortment of rocks
- Glue to paste the rocks together
- Acrylic paint
- Small paintbrushes
- Newspapers to paint on

What you do:

1. The first thing you and your friends will need to do is go out and collect an assortment of rocks. Look for different sizes and unique shapes. You may even discover a rock shaped like an animal that, with a little paint, will look even more like the real thing.

2. After you have collected the rocks, clean and dry them so you can begin painting.

3. Lay the rocks out on newspaper to catch any paint spills. You can glue rocks

together to make animals and other creations, or find a larger rock to paint a fun design on. Then begin painting.

As soon as you're done, set the rocks in a sunny spot and allow to dry completely.

🏀 PLAY IT! Handball

Grassy fields may be hard to find in many parts of the country at this time of year, so opt for a game like handball that can be played on pavement.

The game of handball can be played against a playground wall, a sturdy garage door, or the wall of a building. (Get permission first.) There should be pavement in front of the wall, and you'll need to mark off a square or rectangular area using chalk. (Some parks or playgrounds may have an area that's already marked for handball.)

Two or more players are needed to play the game. You'll also need a handball, or a playground ball. Start by having two players stand inside the chalk boundary. Have one player serve the ball by bouncing it on the ground once, then hitting it against the wall using her hand or fist. After the ball returns and bounces once on the ground, the next player then hits it against the wall with one open hand or fist.

A player is "out" if she misses the ball after it bounces once, hits it so that it bounces outside of the boundaries, or hits the ball on the ground before it hits the wall. After a player is out, she loses her turn and the next player in line gets to join the game. The player who wins becomes the server.

If you have four or more players, you can also play a doubles version of handball. In doubles handball, two teams with two players each play against each other at one time. In this version, either team player can hit the ball after the other team hits it to them.

When a team wins a round, they earn a point and get to serve next. The first team to reach 15 points (or another number you and your friends decide on) wins the game.

WINTER

Chapter Ten

December

December is a great month to . . .

☀ break out the sleds and soar down nearby hills on them.

☀ visit a Christmas tree farm and save a scrawny little tree from being sent to the compost pile. Create homemade decorations to make the little tree shine!

☀ search the neighborhood for the best decorated homes in town. (Check out your local newspaper or community Web site for a listing of great Christmas light displays.)

🏃 DO IT! Put on a Play

Everybody loves a good, heartwarming story, especially around the holidays! Write your own holiday story creating parts for you and your friends, or look through the library for plays, and put on a play for family, friends, and neighbors.

Create a stage for the play, either outdoors or in a garage if the weather is too cold or snowy. Come up with props, like stumps or logs for chairs and cardboard boxes for tables.

Rehearse with your friends until you all feel comfortable with your roles. To let people know about the play, make and hand out flyers to friends and neighbors. Set up chairs — or lay out blankets, pillows, or logs — in front of the stage before the big event.

After all the guests have arrived, let the show begin! Serve apple cider or hot cocoa (see page 91) to your guests after the big event.

🖐 MAKE IT! Popcorn Snowballs

What you need:
- 1 stick of butter, cut in half
- 1 ten-ounce bag mini marshmallows
- 12 cups popped popcorn (unsalted and unbuttered)

Utensils:
- Measuring cups
- Large pot
- Large wooden or heat-proof spoon
- Waxed paper

What you do:

1. Melt half of the stick of butter in a pot over low heat. Add the marshmallows and heat, stirring constantly, until the marshmallows are melted.

2. Remove the pot from the heat and add the popcorn. Stir to coat the popcorn with the marshmallow mixture.

3. Rub the remaining butter on your hands (to keep the mixture from sticking to

them) and then form the popcorn mixture into balls the size of baseballs.

4. Place the balls on sheets of waxed paper to cool and dry.

CREATE IT! Holiday Gift-box Toppers

Use items from nature to decorate wrapped packages for the holidays. Dig through your collection of leaves and pinecones, or go outside and collect holly berries, sprigs of pine needles, twigs, or other things from nature.

Here's what else you will need to make an assortment of festive package toppers:

- Scissors
- Thin ribbon, colored string, thread, or fishing wire
- Silver and gold spray paint
- Hole punch
- Newspaper
- Wrapped packages

To make silver and gold leaves:

1. Use a hole punch to punch holes in the top of each leaf you will be using. Lay the leaves on newspaper.

2. Shake the cans of spray paint well, then spray paint one side of the leaves with either gold or silver paint. Let the leaves dry for about a half hour, then turn them over and spray the other side.

3. After the leaves are completely dry, thread thin ribbon, colored string, thread, or fishing wire through the hole and attach to the ribbon of a wrapped package.

To make pinecone toppers:

1. Either spray paint the pinecones gold or silver on top of the newspaper, or leave them as is. If you paint them, allow them to completely dry for at least one hour.

2. Knot a piece of fishing wire around the base of the pinecone, then use the wire

to attach the pinecone to the ribbon on wrapped packages.

3. In addition, you can tie string onto sprigs of pine needles or holly berries to create pretty package toppers.

🏀 PLAY IT! Holiday Time Treasure Hunt

With so many gifts to give and get during the holiday season, it shouldn't be hard to find treats to hide for a holiday time treasure hunt. In this hunt, it's up to you and your friends to follow clues in order to find the treasure. You can have a grown-up be in charge of coming up with the clues, the hiding places, and the treasure, which can be one wrapped gift, or a bag full of holiday candy, coins, or other toys or treats. Or, you or another friend can take the role of hiding the clues and the treasure.

The game is set up by placing clues throughout the backyard that will help the players get to the treasure. Each clue should lead the players to the next clue. For instance, the first clue, which is given to the players at the start of the game, could read, "Although I don't know how to fly, I often soar high in the sky." With a little thinking and teamwork, the players should be able to figure out that the clue is directing them to a swing. They'd then go to the swing to locate the next clue.

When setting up the game, be sure that the clues and the treasure are well hidden so that none of the players can stumble across them. You may not want to place clues — or the treasure — too close to the other clues. If there's snow on the ground, you can even bury a clue and lead the players to it by telling them how to get there. For instance, the clue might read, "From the back door, take one giant step forward, two giant steps to the left, and four baby steps forward, then dig a little."

Come up with riddles, poems, or clues for each of the hiding spots. The final clue leads the players to the treasure!

Chapter Eleven

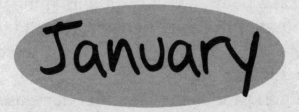
January

January is a great month to . . .

✳ build a snowperson.

✳ visit a local aquarium to get a glimpse of life underwater.

✳ take snowboarding or snow skiing lessons.

✳ plant an herb garden, with plants such as basil, oregano, thyme, sage, and rosemary, so you'll have fresh flavors throughout the winter, and an indoor "summer" garden.

🏃 DO IT! Take a Winter Walk

Don't let a little snow keep you from going on a nature walk! Even during the winter, there are many things to see. Put on layers of warm clothes, and then head outdoors to explore.

During the winter months, it's easy to tell the coniferous trees from the deciduous trees. Conifers, like pine trees, keep their leaves all year long, while deciduous trees, like oaks and elms, shed their leaves for the winter. Collect pinecones and holly berries to use for crafts.

Watch for animal tracks in the snow, and see if you can identify the animals by the tracks they have left. See which animals are brave enough to bear the cold winter months — like squirrels searching for food or deer passing through.

Even though it's cold out, don't forget to bring along bottles of water. You can still become dehydrated in cold and snowy weather.

✋ MAKE IT! Homemade Hot Cocoa

After a cold winter walk, you and a friend will be ready to warm up with a mug of hot homemade cocoa.

What you need:
- 2 cups milk
- 2 teaspoons powdered, unsweetened cocoa
- 2 teaspoons sugar
- Whipped cream or marshmallows (optional)
- A grown-up to help you

Utensils:
- Measuring cups
- Measuring spoons
- Medium-size saucepan
- Wooden or heat-proof spoon
- Two mugs

What you do:

1. Place the milk in the saucepan and heat over medium heat until it is almost boiling. Stir in the cocoa and sugar until they dissolve.

2. Carefully pour the hot cocoa into two mugs and top with whipped cream or marshmallows, if you wish.

Makes 2 servings.

CREATE IT! Tree Bark Rubs

While many trees are left without leaves for the winter, their bark is still in great shape for this fun craft.

The patterns of nature are so unique that they are hard to duplicate. But you can copy the intricate patterns of tree bark by doing these simple rubs.

What you need:

- White paper, such as computer paper
- Chalk or crayons (if using crayons, it's best to remove the paper

wrapping so you can rub them
sideways)
 ◆ Trees

What you do:

1. Pick a tree whose bark is interesting to
   you. The wider the tree, the easier it will
   be for you to make your rubbing.

2. Place the paper on the tree, then rub
   your chalk or crayons over the paper.
   You'll be left with an "imprint" of the
   tree bark.

3. Try rubbing different types and sizes of
   trees. You and your friends can even try
   to figure out which tree you used for
   each of the rubs.

🏀 PLAY IT! Winter Scavenger Hunt

In a scavenger hunt, teams try to be the
first to collect all the items from a list
they've been given. If you have four or
more players, you can form teams of two
or more. If there are two to three players,
you can play against one another.

To hold a scavenger hunt in your yard, it's best to have a grown-up or a friend who won't be playing the game create a list of five items that are easy to find outdoors this time of year. Some items that work well to hunt for include:

- ◆ Pinecones
- ◆ Holly berries
- ◆ Odd-shaped twigs
- ◆ Fallen leaves
- ◆ An icicle
- ◆ A piece of tree bark
- ◆ A lost glove

Be sure that the items on the list can be found in your area. Each team is then given a copy of the list. After someone yells "Go!" the teams try to find all of the items on their list as quickly as possible. The first team to find all the items wins the game.

Chapter Twelve

February

February is a great month to . . .

- *offer to help carry in the firewood — then curl up in cozy chairs by the fireplace and read magazines or your favorite books.*

- *bake a batch of heart-shaped sugar cookie valentines and hand-deliver them to your friends and neighbors.*

- *tune up your bikes (check the brakes, the chains, and fill the tires with air) so you'll be ready to roll when spring comes along!*

👟 DO IT! Go on a Bird-Watching Walk

No matter where you live, February is a great month to look for and feed different types of birds.

During this time of year in the South and warmer states, you will see birds who have migrated down from colder states, such as hummingbirds and warblers. In the north and northeast United States, winter months leave only the hardiest birds who can handle the cold, as well as some winter visitors.

In colder spots, look for birds such as chickadees, finches, woodpeckers, and brightly colored cardinals. Near lakes or ponds, you might find ducks, snow geese, or swans.

Take along a fieldbook about birds to help you identify the ones you spot. Birds will likely "hang out" near bird feeders, so consider making a bird feeder to attract these feathered visitors (see page 98).

Draw pictures of the birds in your journal, and in several months, you can compare your winter bird discoveries with the birds you saw in the summer.

✍ MAKE IT! "Birdseed" Cookies

They may be called birdseed cookies, but these yummy treats definitely aren't for the birds!

What you need:
- ½ cup butter or margarine
- ⅓ cup brown sugar
- 3 tablespoons honey
- 1 cup quick-cooking oats
- ⅓ cup chopped almonds
- ⅓ cup sesame seeds
- A grown-up to help you

Utensils:
- Measuring cups
- Measuring spoons
- Medium-size saucepan
- Large wooden or heat-proof spoon
- 11"×7"×2" baking pan

What you do:

1. Combine butter or margarine, brown sugar, and honey in the saucepan.

2. Heat over low heat, stirring constantly, until the butter or margarine is melted and the sugar is dissolved. Remove from the heat.

3. Add oats, almonds, and sesame seeds and mix well.

4. Press the mixture into the baking pan and let cool.

5. When cooled, slice into 20 evenly cut bars.

   Serves 10 (2 for cookies each person).

CREATE IT! Bird Feeder

Get ready for the birds to return from their summer retreat by creating a bird feeder from an empty milk carton.

What you need:
- Empty, half-gallon paper milk carton
- Stapler

- Hole punch
- Scissors
- Thin but sturdy rope or string
- A ruler
- A tree with sturdy limbs
- Birdseed
- An unsharpened pencil
- A grown-up to help you

What you do:

1. Close the top of the milk carton, then secure it by stapling the sides.

2. Use a hole punch to make a hole about a half inch from the top. Thread one end of the rope or string through the hole and secure by tying a knot.

3. Next, carefully cut 2½-inch square openings on opposite sides of the carton, about three inches from the bottom. You can round the top of the openings if you wish. These will be the doors of the bird feeder.

4. To make a perch for the birds to rest on while they are feeding, punch holes un-

derneath each of the doors. Poke the pencil through both holes.

5. Fill the bottom of the feeder with bird-seed. (You can add more birdseed to the feeder as needed.) Attach the other end of the rope or string to a tree limb by tying a knot around it. Be careful that the feeder is not so low that neighboring cats can get to the birds as they feed.

After the feeder is in place, keep your eye out for birds stopping in to enjoy a free meal!

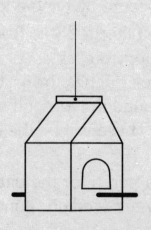

🏀 PLAY IT! Ice-Skating Games

Instead of hibernating in the cold weather, make the most of it by going ice skating with your pals at an outdoor rink. Even if you live in a warm climate, where outdoor ice skating rinks are unheard of, you can still skate by going to an indoor rink.

Nearly all public skating rinks rent skates, so you don't even have to own a pair. Be sure to get skates that fit well, even if it means trying on a few pairs.

Once you and your friends are on the ice, here are a few games you can play.

Skate Trains

Form a line and have each skater hold the skater in front of her at the hips. Skate around the rink, trying to stay attached at the hips. Take turns being the leader.

Doubles Races

Have skaters form pairs. Have each pair join together by holding hands (one of each skating pair will have to skate backward), then race around the rink and see which team can cross the finish line first.

Skate Your Names

Have skaters try and "write" their names on the ice as they skate.

Gliding Contest

Designate two starting lines — one to start skating for speed and another to begin gliding. Have each skater begin skating at the first starting line. When she reaches the second starting line, have her glide on one foot to see how far she can go. Mark the spot and then let the other skaters see if they can glide farther. The one who glides the farthest forward wins.

CONCLUSION

As you can see in this book, there's so much to take advantage of in the great outdoors. Celebrate nature every opportunity you get. Explore your surroundings, and get inspired by nature to come up with more outdoor games and activities. Even when you can't be outdoors, you can have fun indoors with crafts, recipes, games, and activities inspired by nature. With good friends close by, whatever you do is bound to be fun!